Railway Byways in Yorkshire

by
Ronald Nelson Redman

Dalesman Books
1979

£1.75

The Dalesman Publishing Company Ltd.,
Clapham (via Lancaster), North Yorkshire

First published 1979

ISBN: 0 85206 556 6

Printed in Great Britain by Galava Printing Company Limited,
Hallam Road, Nelson, Lancashire

Contents

The cover illustrations show:- Front: **Joem** and train at Layerthorpe on the Derwent Valley Railway (R. Bastin); Back—top: Scarborough North Bay Railway **Neptune** at the Leeds works of Hudswell Clarke for rebuilding (author's collection); Back—bottom: **Blythe** prepares to depart from Pateley Bridge on the Nidd Valley Railway in 1928 (H.G.W. Household).

Introduction

THE light and narrow gauge railways of this country have always attracted a dedicated following of enthusiasts, and since main line steam power has all but vanished from the scene, the present wave of nostalgia for more leisurely days has created a new interest in railway byways, coupled to the mania for railway preservation.

In the restricted space of the following publication, one can hardly do more than scratch the surface of the history of the minor lines of England's largest county. Yorkshire has a rich railway past from the introduction of Matthew Murray's pioneer steam locomotive in 1812 on the Middleton Colliery line near Leeds, to the re-introduction of steam as a summer tourist attraction on the Derwent Valley Railway at York, the last truly independent light railway which originally ended its regular passenger service as long ago as 1926.

Most of the lines covered have long since closed, but as they were generally located in attractive areas, visits to the remains can be recommended as a rewarding experience, particularly if made on a warm summer day. My wife and I covered most of them at 'blackberry time' and enjoyed killing two birds with one stone.

Ronald Nelson Redman,
Horsforth, Leeds.

Acknowledgements

ONE could fill pages thanking all who have made helpful suggestions, loaned photographs or walked miles with me along old track beds as we tried to capture the lost magic of the little railways at home and overseas.

Pride of place must go to Kenneth E. Hartley, the doyen of Yorkshire light railway enthusiasts, who has personally recorded in detail the history of many of the lines included. Ken has generously placed at my disposal his encyclopaedic knowledge of the subject as well as many of his historic negatives, and without his assistance, the project could not have been so comprehensive.

My grateful thanks are also due to the following friends and organisations for their valued assistance:-

Clarksons of York, Cleveland Transit, E.G. Cope, Glen Enterprises Ltd., P.S. Halton, H. Holdsworth, G. Horsman, A. Kinsey, A. Neale, The Narrow Gauge Railway Society Library, The Railway Preservation Society, T. Stanhope, J.W. Steel, I. Stephenson and M. Swift.

1. The Light Railways

LIGHT railways were a product of the last 25 years of the 19th century and the first 12 years of this century. Their concept is best described by a leading exponent E.R. Calthrop, M. Inst. C.E., M.I.M.E., in his writings of 1904 as: 'The fundamental idea of light railway construction and working is the elimination of every kind of expenditure which is non-essential to its efficiency as a means of transport, and the reduction of all permanent way, works, plant, and appliances to their simplest and most inexpensive forms.'

Historically, they are the most colourful and interesting of the minor railways, and were all built with the intention of providing a regular passenger service. Improved roads and bus services over the years forced them to lapse into freight only lines but in their time, they provided the only means of transport in thinly populated areas.

The Easingwold Railway

THIS classic independent standard gauge light railway served the needs of an agricultural community well for 66 fairly successful years, until December, 1957. The single track line connected the attractive old-world market town of Easingwold, 13 miles north of York, with Alne, on the North Eastern Railway's main line, the run being a modest single track of two miles, 37 chains, which made it in its day the shortest standard gauge passenger railway in the British Isles.

Opening day came on Saturday, 25th July, 1891, with all the

pomp inevitably associated with such occasions and the directors treated about 400 local schoolchildren and teachers to free return trips on four special trains, followed by tea in the Easingwold Market Hall. It was a day for all to remember when the local two-horse omnibus, which had provided the thrice a day service between the two centres, was put out of business by the new iron horse in the shape of a shiny new four-coupled saddle tank, coupled to two elderly secondhand coaches.

The line had experienced considerable and protracted birth pains before it became a reality; a line in the area had been mooted way back in 1838 but the Easingwold Railway was not incorporated until 27th August, 1887, after an Act to construct the line had been passed. The four local worthies who formed the Board of Directors put economy of construction at the top of their list of priorities and convinced themselves that the new railway could be built and equipped for £10,000. They should have felt some trepidation when they awarded the contract for the construction to a company called Death & Co., and this rather morbid sounding enterprise 'passed away' with the line only half built. Another contractor whose name is not recorded was called in to finish the job almost four years after the inaugural meeting, and by the end the cost had escalated to £17,000.

From Monday, the 27th July, 1891, the railway started to settle down to normal revenue earning business with nine trains a day in each direction on weekdays, but the peace of the Sabbath was never shattered by the sound of steam trains on the Easingwold line. As most trains were passenger service only, the journey time allowed, which never altered over the years, was eight minutes in each direction. This did however tend to change when heavy freight was to hand and goods wagons had to be tucked in between the engine and coaches to form a mixed train.

Despite never having excessive funds to play with, the directors did see fit to purchase new locomotives over the years and had a distinct liking for the products of the Leeds based Railway Foundry of Hudswell Clarke & Co. Ltd. The first one for the opening of the line was a tiny 0-4-0 saddle tank weighing only 15 tons 6 cwt. in full working order. It left the Jack Lane Works of the builders on 24th June, 1891, with an invoice for £670. Being essentially a light industrial shunting design it proved to be a bit underpowered and, as the Board of Trade took exception to the use of four-coupled locomotives in passenger service, it was soon returned to Leeds to be re-sold into industrial service.

Its place was taken by a six-coupled Hudswell saddle tank, which carried a brass nameplate **Easingwold**, on 20th August, 1891, and until early 1903, when she was re-sold, this locomotive took over the full railway service. The last new locomotive was the famous and long lived No. 2, another Hudswell of slightly more powerful performance which represented a standard 13in cylinder design, very popular with other light railways and contractors around the country, and at a cost of £1,185 it gave sterling service up to 1946, returning briefly to its Leeds birthplace on three occasions for repairs or rebuilding.

After the decision was reluctantly made to scrap No. 2, in 1947, after the Darlington locomotive works engineer had presented the directors with an estimate for £1,400 to re-boiler and overhaul the veteran, and the cost of good secondhand industrial locomotives was adjusted too high, the only alternative was to hire motive power. From that time to the end of the railway, the London & North Eastern Railway and later British Railways provided engines, often a drain on the slim resources when they were pushed to find hire charges of over £40 per week.

In later years the locomotives used were always 0-6-0 side tanks of the J71 or J72 class, and how they differed from the gleaming old No. 2 with their drab black livery—most were elderly machines, and looked it! Their condition was not helped by the fact that despite being small engines by main line standards, they were still too big to fit into the tiny Easingwold locomotive shed, and had to stand permanently outside.

On the coaching side, the company was never so free with its money, and it was vintage secondhand vehicles all the way. For the opening, two obsolete North Eastern Railway four-wheel coaches made up the train, their nearly flat roofs set off by luggage rails. These were retired and converted into huts about 1903 to be replaced by three four-wheelers which had seen service on the North London Railway.

Six-wheel stock came on the scene after the 1st World War, but both coaches soon had their central wheels removed to form long wheelbase four-wheel vehicles, and in this form they lasted up to 1930 during which time they were kept in a smart medium brown livery with grey roofs. Their eventual replacement was a single ex North Eastern six-wheeler, which was allowed to retain all its wheels up to 1946 when the sole surviving passenger coach arrived on the line, a very vintage six-wheel, 1st and 2nd class brake composite of Great Central Railway parentage. This old timer slowly started to get more down at heel, for the rest of its days on the Easingwold until the passenger service packed up for good in November 1948, by which time little paintwork remained, and the upholstery, particularly in the 2nd class, was badly torn. Despite its very rough looks it managed to continue in service as a parcels van until 1956, when it was thankfully purchased for private preservation and moved for storage to the nearby Derwent Valley Railway.

Freight stock was never a problem, as main line wagons were used, and the only trouble really was that the volume of traffic could hardly have ever reached the backers' optimistic expectations, from the first freight recorded in July 1897, when horses were moved to the Malton Show, right through to the general agricultural products of sugar beet and potatoes that filled the odd wagons in later years.

The only boom time for the line was during the last war when No. 2 trundled thousands of tons of munitions to Easingwold for storage and, at the end of hostilities, 40,000 tons in the opposite direction for dumping. The prosperity was short-lived, and the track degenerated into a very rough state and had to be completely renewed in 1944/45—the cost was the last nail in the coffin. Not surprisingly, No. 2 was completely worn out and during 1946 the line temporarily closed due to lack of motive power.

Freight re-started with hired locomotives and dragged on until the final curtain call on 27th December, 1957, when J72 No. 68698, with 'City of Tears' chalked on the side tanks and 'Omega' on the smoke-box, hauled the last train to Alne where driver George Paragreen, with 40 years' experience behind him, dropped the fire for the last time and had to get a lift home by car. One nice touch to this sad occasion had been the attendance of Mr. Sidney Smith on the footplate for the last run. Mr. Smith, the son of one of the original directors, had had the privilege of driving the first train on opening day way back in 1891.

Little remains of this charming little line to interest the enthusiast. The station site at Alne has been totally obliterated—not even a platform remains where now the main line high speed trains flash through at speeds unheard of in the old days.

Easingwold is still worth a visit, if only for the attractive architecture in the old town centre, but the station site is difficult to locate, apart from the remaining Station Hotel which dates back to 1892. One could easily miss the station yard area, now covered by a new housing development, appropriately called 'Station Court'. In contrast to the very modern buildings is the old engine shed which still remains at the rear of the site—a tiny brick building standing in long grass, looking more like a rather old domestic garage.

The works plate from the old No. 2 was passed to York Railway Museum and is now presumably in the National Collection, but the most tangible remains are the ex Great Central coach, purchased by Mr. J.H. Bowles and stored on the Derwent Valley Railway. It was acquired by the Railway Preservation Society for £25 and moved by road to Chasewater in December 1968 for restoration to its original G.C.R. condition and livery. Ten years later, the rebuilding work was well advanced when vandals struck, the coack was broken into, fittings removed and the brake end set alight. Fortunately, the firemen's strike had just ended and the fire was contained to one end, although about 40 per cent of the coach was badly damaged.

Despite this terrible affair, unfortunately so typical of the days we now live in, work has recommenced on the re-restoration of this interesting vehicle, assisted by a grant from the Transport Trust, and we can in time look forward to seeing the coach in service on the Chasewater Light Railway.

The Cawood, Wistow and Selby Light Railway

THIS interesting little country byway probably had the longest title of any of the county's light railways, but it only enjoyed a brief period of independence. In many ways it had similarities to the Easingwold Railway, being basically an agricultural carrier in an area that to this day remains thinly populated. Like so many of the country's light railways, it did not have the look of a passenger line but such things did not deter the brave railway promoters of old.

Its origins date back to an ambitious scheme proposed in 1882 which failed to gain sufficient support in the area, but by 1884, a single track connecting Cawood to Selby was settled for, and the contract for building the line was awarded to the Horsforth, near Leeds, contractors, Messrs. Whitaker Brothers. The first sod-cutting ceremony took place on 11th July, 1896, and the official opening day—rather marred by very cold and windy conditions—came on 16th February, 1898. The directors' special on the day was arranged to carry 200 passengers so the line's two coaches had to be augmented by several North Eastern Railway vehicles, a fair load for the company's little 0-6-0 ST locomotive **Cawood**.

The five mile line started at Brayton Gates, later known as Selby West, at the junction with the North Eastern Railway's Leeds to Selby line. The station was something of a temporary affair with a wooden platform and shelter. Hopes had been entertained that the independent line's trains would be able to work into Selby station but agreement could not be reached with the main line company. In point of fact, neither of the stations was near the town centre and were about a mile apart. Brick built stations of a more permanent nature were provided at Wistow (3 miles) and at Cawood, and the junction had a brick engine shed of very generous proportions for the line's single locomotive. With the very flat agricultural landscape of the area, very few features occurred en route apart from the inevitable gated crossings over the country roads. The only engineering job was the plate girder bridge over the wide stream known as the 'Selby Dam', just after the Selby/Leeds road crossing.

Time allowed for the run was 17 minutes, and the initial service provided for five trains a day in each direction. Fares were low, based on a penny a mile for 3rd class and threepence for 1st class splendour. Specials were arranged to suit demand, a popular working being in connection with the Leeds pantomime seasons when the fare for the return journey was a very modest 1s. 3d (6½p). Unlike most light railways, mixed trains were never operated apart from the working of empty coaching stock. Freight could be fairly heavy and the regular morning goods could be expected to run to 20 wagons of potatoes, and large quantities of sugar beet provided good freight revenue.

The independent line's only locomotive **Cawood** was a typical product of the famous Boyne Engine Works of Manning Wardle & Co. of Leeds. This carried Works No. 1360 of 1897 and basically it was one of the firm's Class L 0-6-0 saddle tank designs, with inside cylinders 12 ins x 18 ins and driving wheels 3 ft 6 ins diameter and scaled just over 20 tons in full working order. The engine and rolling stock were obtained on a hire agreement with the Yorkshire Railway Wagon Co. Records have not survived of the two coaches but it is probable they could have been secondhand ex North Eastern Railway six-wheel stock.

Despite the railway's light construction it obviously attracted a fair amount of attention from its wealthy neighbour, the North Eastern Railway, who lost no time in purchasing the complete line on 1st January, 1900, for the sum of £32,000, and immediately took over the working of the branch. The temporary station at Brayton Gate lasted up to 1st July, 1904, when sense at last prevailed and trains were allowed to run through into Selby. The Manning locomotive and stock were replaced in 1901 by main line equipment, the first locomotive being the North Eastern Railway 0-6-0 class H2, No. 407, which soon became a near permanent feature on the branch up to the summer of 1912. It is interesting to note that No. 407 eventually finished up in industrial service and ended its life on the famous Middleton Colliery line in Leeds, where it lasted until the late 1940s.

Various forms of interesting motive power rolled over the Cawood line through the years, starting with two Napier-powered 48 seater petrol electric autocars Nos. 3170 and 3171, built in 1902, and used for a time on summer services between Scarborough and Filey. They put Cawood on the map for a time with the 8.52 a.m. departure from the branch terminus working right through to the city of York. These two fine railcars lasted until the late 1920s when the line reverted to steam prior to the arrival on the scene in July 1923 of the N.E.R. converted Leyland road bus No. 110, virtually a 35 h.p. 26 seat petrol bus running on flanged wheels. It was first shown, finished in N.E.R. teak, at the 1925 Darlington Centenary Exhibition. It was to put in a lot of good work in the Selby area up to 11th November, 1926, when it came to a sad end being engulfed by fire whilst being refuelled at Selby and damaged beyond repair.

A steam auto-train service followed but was soon replaced by the famous Sentinel-Cammell steam rail coaches. The L.N.E.R. had started with two of the vertically-boilered Sentinel cars in East Anglia in 1925, and two years later ordered two more of improved design to accommodate 65 passengers each. Someone in high places hit on the brilliant idea of naming the cars after the old stage-coaches, a stroke of genius that provided a lot of colourful names for the fleet of railcars to come, such as **Tally Ho**, and **High Flyer**. **Brilliant**, No. 6524, had trials in Yorkshire during 1927 and attained a speed of 50 m.p.h. between York and Malton; soon 20 more were on order to be followed by a further 39 with the engines increased from two to six cylinders. The two Sentinels to see most service on the Cawood branch were **True Blue** and **Trafalgar**, and these eventually saw out the end of the passenger service which packed up on the last day of December, 1929.

Freight services carried on with conventional steam providing the driving force with classes J71(E), J72(E1) and J77 doing the honours until the line finally closed on 23rd May, 1960, but to complete the very varied collection of locomotives that saw service on this branch, for the last month or so a 204 h.p. six-coupled diesel shunter from Selby yard moved the very light trains and D2063 worked an enthusiasts' special on 22nd April. The track was lifted and the bridge that had caused all the weight restrictions for the line was dismantled during 1961, the most tangible remains now being some buildings, including gatehouses at Haxley Lane, Selby Common and Broad Lane. Wistow station has been converted into a nice bungalow, with the weigh office and goods shed still there too. Cawood station retains all its buildings, but no platform or loading bank, and over the years has started to look a bit worse for wear.

The Nidd Valley Light Railway

PROBABLY the finest of Yorkshire's light railways, both for its setting in the wild and windy scenery of upper Nidderdale under the shadow of Great Whernside, and for a very interesting stud of locomotives, the Nidd Valley Railway was unique in being a passenger carrying line worked by a municipality. If only it could have lasted to more recent times, it would surely have been a prime candidate for a preservation project.

The crowds that flock to the attractive little town of Pateley Bridge over summer weekends little realise that this market town once had two railway stations served by two different railways. The first line to reach Nidderdale was the 14 mile Pateley branch of the North Eastern Railway which connected the valley to Harrogate, 12 miles away by road, the first train running on 15th May, 1862. It was not until the turn of the century that another railway was proposed when a company entitled Power & Traction Ltd made an application for authority to build a 2 ft 6 in gauge light railway from Pateley Bridge to Lofthouse, a tiny village some seven miles up the valley. The application was successful, but the necessary capital to build the railway was not forthcoming and in 1904 Bradford Corporation arranged to take over the authority, on 1st March, and changed the gauge to standard, but of light proportions (the rail to be of 56 lb. per yard flat bottomed profile). Work soon commenced on the construction of the new railway after the first sod had been ceremoniously cut in July 1904 by Alderman Holdsworth.

Bradford Corporation only wanted the line to supply materials to the construction site of the Angram reservoir and dam, but to comply with the Light Railway Act it had to provide a passenger and freight service between Lofthouse and Pateley. The main site at Angram was seven miles further up to the head of Nidderdale from Lofthouse, and this section was first served by a private road laid on land purchased by Bradford Corporation. However, no road could carry the volume of materials required, and the line was extended by the side of the road right through for a total of nearly 14 miles from Pateley Bridge, a journey that took a full hour. The first Corporation project near Pateley had been the 1,610 million gallon Gowthwaite reservoir started in 1893 and brought into service in 1901; the second phase of the project, the

110 acre Angram job, was on a large scale with the water held back by a dam 1,000 ft long and a maximum height of 120 ft.

The completed railway climbed all the way from Pateley Bridge, but above Lofthouse the grades were formidable with long stretches of 1 in 40 and included a 180 yard tunnel cut through solid limestone, the spoil of which made good ballast for the track. The passenger section had four stations—Pateley Bridge; Wath, 1½ miles out; Ramsgill, 4½ miles out; and Lofthouse. The station at Pateley was a ten minute walk from the North Eastern branch terminus but a connection was built in for goods traffic transfer. When the passenger service of four trains a day commenced on the 12th September, 1907, the day after the official opening by the then Lord Mayor of Bradford, Alderman J.A. Godwin, with fares of 2s. 1st class and 1s. 2nd class (10p and 5p), it had two very interesting locomotives named **Holdsworth** and **Milner** which carried N.V.R. Nos. 1 and 2. They had originally been Metropolitan Railway Nos. 20 and 34, and were purchased after restoration at the Metropolitan's Neasden Works. They were both classic 4-4-0 tank locomotives built by Beyer, Peacock & Co. for underground service in 1866 and 1879 respectively. Their useful life in London was coming to an end due to the expansion of the electrification of the underground system. Neasden Works removed the condensing apparatus and fitted all-over cabs before they headed north via York. They retained their distinctive red livery but had the addition of the Bradford coat-of-arms and their new names.

The Metropolitan also supplied the first coaches to the line, a set of ten elderly four-wheeled vehicles, the only new coach purchased being a very impressive open balcony directors' saloon built by Hurst Nelson. Despite the good trackwork and solid road-bed the engines were to prove too heavy for the light rail and **Milner** was re-sold in 1909 and saw service on a quarry line near Penmaenmawr, when its place was taken by a new **Milner**, an 0-6-0 tank locomotive built by Hudswell Clarke & Co. Ltd. to their Works No. 882, in May, 1909, at a cost of £1,330. It was fitted with outside 12 in x 18 in cylinders and 3 ft 3½ in diameter wheels, weighed 30½ tons in full working order and was more to the liking of the railway, as opposed to the 46½ tons of the 4-4-0 tank locomotive.

Holdsworth went on to put in a lot of good work up and down the valley on 20 minute journeys, but was finally scrapped in 1920, its place being taken the following year by another rare piece of equipment, an ex Great Western Railway steam railcar originally built by Kerr Stuart to their Works No. 906 in 1905, with the 48-seater passenger body section by Hurst Nelson. The power bogie had outside 9 in x 15 in cylinders, 3 ft 3 in wheels and the boiler which worked at 160 p.s.i. was mounted transversely. Full control arrangements were also provided at the opposite end of the car, and in keeping with the practice of naming locomotives after Bradford worthies the new 60 ft long railcar was named **Hill** after the then Lord Mayor.

In its heyday the Nidd Valley Railway was a very efficient undertaking with five passenger trains a day in each direction, supplemented by three workmen's trains. Many other locomotives worked over the line on goods traffic and these will be listed at the end of the section. Notable amongst these were two heavy 0-6-0 saddle tank engines, **Gadie** by Andrew Barclay & Co. Ltd., maker's No. 1866 of 1925, and **Blythe** from the Avonside Engine Co. Ltd., their No. 1894 of 1922. These worked the heavy through trains from Pateley carrying cement, coal and the like to the working sites. Smaller saddle tank engines acted as shunting and contractors' locomotives in the stone quarry and in the workings of the Corporation's contractor, John Best of Edinburgh.

John Watson was the Waterworks Engineer for the Corporation and he was responsible for the actual construction and for making sure that the work was up to standard and costs were not getting out of hand. He reported to the chairman and Waterworks Committee on 30th May, 1917, that the original estimate for the Angram project by John Best was £365,492 16s 6d, and pointed out that the reservoir was full and overflowing in January 1916 and the work nearly completed. John Best had died but his sons carried on the works which were completed on 6th September, 1916, at a total cost of £372,760 2s 6d, just £7,267 6s 0d over the original estimate—£3,439 16s 0d was for extras ordered by the Corporation so the actual extra cost was £2,827 10s 0d, less than 0.8% and they proposed they should be paid. The committee was delighted with the work and paid up, passing a resolution that an honorarium of £200 be given to Mr. W.T. Croft, the Assistant Town Clerk, who had acted as secretary and manager to the Nidd Valley line in addition to his other duties.

Work started on the Nidderdale third phase in October, 1921, the building of the last great reservoir at Scar House where 2,200 million gallons of water with a surface area of 172 acres were to be retained by a dam containing one million tons of concrete and masonry, the carriageway on the top of the dam to be 1,578 ft long by 135 ft wide at its maximum point. The task was so vast that a complete village had to be built for the labour force of 700 men, and 13 locomotives, 25 locomotive cranes and four steam navvies were involved in the project. The railway had to feed the site, apart from the stone for the dam which was quarried in the hills to the north of the valley at a height of 500 ft above the dam, and a double road incline was built to bring the millstone grits down to the dressing yards, later to be moved by locomotive to the actual site.

Once the work was completed at Angram, the railhead was cut

Easingwold Railway—1. Scene at the turn of the century. Locomotive No. 1 Easingwold with the original vintage ex North Eastern Railway 4-wheel coaches in Easingwold Station. (Mrs. M. Coates c/o K.E. Hartley's collection)

High summer 1937—all the atmosphere of those pre-war light railway days caught in this study of Easingwold No. 2, slumbering in Alne station with the Saturday afternoon train. (K. E. Hartley)

Easingwold Railway—2. Only a tiny engine by main line standards, J71 No. 8297 was still too tall to enter Easingwold engine shed and had to 'sleep' outside after the day's work on 20th September, 1948. (K. E. Hartley)

The end of the line—just about ready for firewood, the ex North London coach at the rear of the Easingwold engine shed. Replaced in 1921, it had reached this state by June, 1950. It ended up as lighting up material for the locomotive in 1953, surely a fitting cremation for an old coach. (K. E. Hartley)

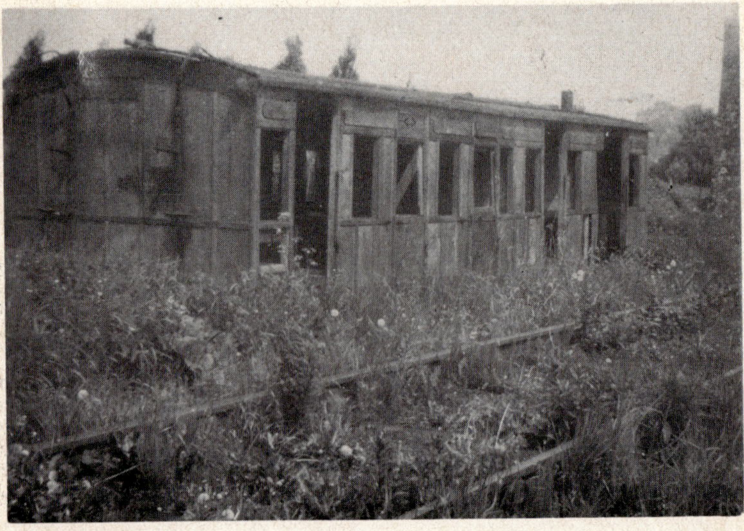

Easingwold Railway—3. The last year of passenger service in 1948 saw the ex Great Central 1st & 2nd class coach getting a bit down at heel. Internally only the 1st class was fit to travel in but soon it would only be required for parcel traffic. (R. N. Redman)

The popular light railway and contractors 13in type by Hudswell Clarke & Co. could stand up to a lot of use and abuse over the years, particularly this one, Easingwold Railway No. 2. (Author's collection)

Cawood, Wistow & Selby Light Railway.
Above: J77 0-6-0 No. 68406 with the Cawood branch daily goods crossing the dam bridge on April 10th, 1952. (K. E. Hartley)

Opposite top: Directors and shareholders of the Cawood Wistow & Selby Light Railway pose in front of their Manning Wardle 0-6-0 ST Cawood and N.E.R. coach in late Autumn 1897, a few months prior to the official opening at Broad Lane Gates. (Author's collection)

Opposite, bottom: J77 0-6-0 No. 68406 shunts the branch train at Cawood in June 1953. (K. E. Hartley)

68406

Nidd Valley Light Railway—1. Despite the title of light railway, the Nidd Valley did not skimp on its structures as is evidenced from this interesting shot of the construction of Ramsgill station. (Collection T. Garth)

Ramsgill station in its completed form. Note the open lever frame on the station platform. (Author's collection)

Nidd Valley Light Railway—2. Light railway track-laying in progress at Lofthouse station. In this obviously posed photograph, the onlookers far outnumber the actual tracklayers. (Collection T. Garth)

September 11th, 1907, opening day of the Nidd Valley Light. The Lord Mayor of Bradford and his party stand by their official saloon coach coupled to the rear of the ex-Metropolitan Railway coaches at Scar House Village station. (Collection T. Garth)

Nidd Valley Light Railway—3.

Above: No. 1. Holdsworth en route from the Metropolitan Railway's Neasden works to Pateley Bridge. Photographed in superb condition outside the old York roundhouse. (Author's collection)

Opposite, top: The Hudswell tank locomotive Milner in near new condition circa 1910. Worthy of note is the number of uniformed railway personnel. (Author's collection)

Opposite, bottom: Steam railcar Hill. Built by Kerr Stuart, it formerly worked on the Great Western Railway. (Author's collection)

Nidd Valley Light Railway—4. A Passenger train stands in Lofthouse Station in 1928 with locomotive Milner blowing off. (H.G.W. Household)

Bradford Corporation's private inspection car built by Hurst Nelson and lettered Nidd Railway. (Author's collection)

Nidd Valley Light Railway—5. Manning Wardle built locomotive Haig with a typical contractors' side tipping wagon of wooden construction on the Scar House contract. (Collection T. Garth)

Gadie heads Illingworth on a Scar House Reservoir bound train of contractors' wagons. Note the large wooden 'dumb' buffers on Gadie—standard practice of the period on many contractors' locomotives. (Collection T. Garth)

Derwent Valley Railway—1. Not a sleeper in sight as B.R. 65714 shunts the daily goods over the grass grown tracks at Wheldrake station in August, 1959. (R. N. Redman)

The Derwent Valley line always had distinctive and well maintained stations. Typical is Thorganby, photographed on 4th August, 1959. (R. N. Redman)

Derwent Valley Railway—2. The railway's Sentinel geared steam locomotive of 1925 on a freight working in Layerthorpe station, a view which was used by the locomotive builders in their catalogue along with a reminder that it cost £1,400 new and saved the light railway £1,600 in its first year! (H. G.W. Household)

A typical daily goods train complete with the ex-South Eastern & Chatham Railway 6-wheel brake van. Photographed 8th August, 1959. (R. N. Redman)

Sand Hutton Light Railway—1. Miniature railway Bassett-Lowke Synolda with test train circa 1913/14 in Sand Hutton Hall grounds. (K. E. Hartley collection)

Sir Robert Walker at the controls of Synolda, named after his first wife, the central figure in the coach. (K. E. Hartley collection)

Sand Hutton Light Railway—2. Synolda with train of 4-wheel open coaches at the Garden Station and coach shed. (K. E. Hartley collection)

Hunslet 0-4-0 WT Esme on train coupled to the Hudson bogie saloon. With Sir Robert and Lady Esme Walker are George Batty on the locomotive and Arthur Robinson the guard at the left. (K. E. Hartley collection)

Sand Hutton Light Railway—3. Hunslet 0-4-0 WT No. 11 shunting at Sand Hutton Depot in early 1932. (K. E. Hartley)

Builders' photograph of the Sand Hutton brake and parcels van. 15 ft long and with a 6 ft wheelbase, this was quite a vehicle for the 18 in gauge when supplied in 1923. (Robert Hudson Ltd)

back to Scar House, four miles above Lofthouse. Passenger traffic was heavy at times and plenty of workmen's trains had to go up to the top site and work the old four-wheeled ex-Metropolitan coaches, now relegated to this service. **Blythe** was fitted with a footplate-mounted high-speed reciprocating steam engine and dynamo for lighting the train. The normal passenger coach stock had been improved by the purchase of 12 four-wheel coaches from the Maryport & Carlisle Railway. The year 1923 was a good one for the line with traffic growth and the balance sheet ended with a clear profit of £4,000, but then a slow decline set in, once road transport started to make a more marked effect, and eventually the Corporation succeeded in obtaining an order to close the railway for public passenger and goods traffic from the last day of December, 1929.

The railway still had a big job to finish and regular workmen's and supply trains ran until the Scar House reservoir was completed. The official opening took place on 7th September, 1936, and the last trains ran not long afterwards. Track lifting started in 1937 and the rail was sold in February, peace returning to Pateley on Saturday evenings after many rowdy scenes had accompanied the last navvies' train back to the contractors' site village after 'closing time'. The last sad act came on 16th June, 1937, with the auction of plant, and pride of place went to the nine locomotives still left at that time. Four by Hudswell Clarke & Co. Ltd. had amongst them **Milner**—despite being rebuilt in 1921 it sold for only £650. Three Manning Wardles and one Peckett all brought less than £700 each, but the Barclay of 1925 was sold for the record sum of £1,000.

Little remains of this fascinating railway today. Ramsgill and Wath stations are now detached houses and the track bed can still be traced in places, and worth visiting is a good photographic display on view at the new Pateley Bridge Museum. The most unusual survivor was the remains of **Hill**, the steam railcar, which was sold for scrap after the passenger service closed and more than 30 years later its remains still languished in Robinson & Birdsell's scrapyard in Leeds, the coach still complete with G.W.R. notices and fittings—another interesting relic which escaped the preservation net. Pateley Bridge lost its railway connection via the branch to Harrogate when the line closed to goods traffic in November, 1964, the passenger services having given in to road competition on 31st March, 1951.

Nidd Valley Light Railway: List of Locomotives used on the Railway and Construction Work

Name	Makers	Works No.	Date	Type	Cylinders	Driving Wheels
No. 1 Holdsworth	Beyer Peacock	707	1866	4-4-0T	oc17in x 24in	5ft - 9in
No. 2 Milner	Beyer Peacock	1878	1879	,,	,,	,,
Milner	Hudswell Clarke	882	1909	0-6-0T	oc12in x 18in	3ft - 3½in
Hill	Kerr Stuart	906	1905	0-4-0 (railcar)	oc9in x 15in	3ft - 3in
Blythe	Avonside	1894	1922	0-6-0ST	oc14½x20in	,,
Gadie	Andrew Barclay	1866	1925	,,	oc14in x 22in	3ft - 5in
Mitchell	Hudswell Clarke	1208	1916	,,	oc14in x 20in	3ft - 7in
Watson	,, ,,	1197	,,	,,	,,	,,
Craven	,, ,,	1411	1920	,,	,,	,,
Ian Hamilton	,, ,,	480	1897	,,	oc13in x 18in	3ft - 0½in
Haig	Manning Wardle	1224	1891	,,	ic13in x 20in	3ft - 3in
Allenby	,, ,,	1379	1898	,,	ic13in x 18in	3ft - 0in
Beatty	,, ,,	1669	1905	,,	,,	,,
Trotter	Andrew Barclay	1810	1925	0-4-0ST	oc10in x 18in	,,
Stringer	,, ,,	1877	1925	,,	,,	,,
Kitchener	Peckett	939	1902	0-6-0ST	oc14in x 20in	3ft - 6in

In addition two 2ft 0in gauge battery powered locomotives were used on tunnel construction work.

The Derwent Valley Railway

KNOWN as the Derwent Valley Light Railway until 1973, this is one independent line that has proved the exception to the rule with no rusting old tracks and balance sheets continually in the red. The D.V.R. is one line, admittedly much reduced in length over the years, which on its remaining section is very much alive and doing very good business.

Like so many of the independent lines the railway took a long time to come into being, starting with two Rural District Councils applying for a Light Railway Order in 1899. Intended from the start to be mainly an agricultural branch connecting York (Layerthorpe) station on the east of the city and Cliff Common on the Selby-Market Weighton line, a distance of 16 miles, construction got underway in 1911. The first section of 7 miles to Wheldrake was opened for freight only in October, 1912, the full line being officially opened by the Lady Deramore who cut the tape to set off the first passenger train from Layerthorpe on 21st July, 1913.

To avoid possible competition, the line entered into an agreement with the North Eastern Railway to hire motive power from the main line company in return for which 'big brother' was not to operate omnibuses or lorries in the vicinity of the light railway. A N.E.R. 2-2-4T, No. 1679, worked the inaugural train but normal services were usually in the hands of an aged Fletcher 0-6-0T which soon settled in to work the services of three mixed trains a day, booked to cover the line in 'more or less' 50 minutes. Passenger traffic built up for only two short years using two ex N.E.R. six-wheel carriages repainted in the company's dark blue livery. The peak year for ticket sales was 1915 when nearly 50,000 people were carried but then a slow decline set in and the service fizzled out in 1926, apart from the occasional 'Blackberry Specials' or excursion trains which ran from 1928 until 1932.

At the end of the first hire agreement, the new post-war hire rates proposed by the N.E.R. were out of the question for the D.V.L.R.'s slim funds but a novel solution was found to reduce expenses. The passenger traffic was entrusted to two four-wheel Ford powered rail buses usually coupled back-to-back. These lightweight vehicles had bodies manufactured by C.G. Roe Ltd., of Leeds, each bus seating 36 passengers. In service, it was usual practice for the leading car to haul the other, running in neutral gear. Running costs fell from 1s 5d (7p) per mile with steam to approximately 5d (2p), but the reduction in passengers was even more dramatic and the service was withdrawn in September, 1926, the two rail buses to see service again after re-gauging on the 3 ft 0 in gauge system of the County Donegal Joint Committee in Ireland.

For freight traffic, the life blood of any railway, novel forms of motive power were experimented with, starting in September, 1923, when the Four-wheel Drive Co. of Slough delivered a light 36 h.p. petrol locomotive. The design was virtually a development of a four-wheel drive road lorry incorporating a wooden cab and a rear open type wagon body. It had a month's trial on the D.V.L.R. but was grossly underpowered for the work required and was soon returned to the manufacturers. Far more successful for a time was the introduction of a 100 h.p. 22 ton **Sentinel** four-wheel vertically-boilered geared locomotive for a total cost of £1,400 in 1925. For many years, the main line railways used the Sentinel Patent designs but it was the tiny D.V.L.R. which showed the way after the L.N.E.R. had carried out dynamometer car tests to determine that the light locomotive could in fact move around 500 tons on the level at 1¾ m.p.h. Haulage costs per mile were of prime importance to the light railway and, over a month, tests indicated a reduction of costs per train mile to 9d (3.75p) against an average of 1s 4d (6.6p) for a hired locomotive.

It is ironic that once the passenger service was abandoned the freight side started to pick up and the tiny Sentinel could not cope with the heavy trains of over 50 wagons which became a common occurrence by late 1927. There was nothing for it but to negotiate a new hire agreement with the L.N.E.R. who were soon shedding a Fletcher 0-4-4T at Layerthorpe during weekdays, the D.V.L.R. to provide coal and footplate crew. During the Second World War, and after, a series of 'J' class 0-6-0 types plus the occasional W.D. saddle tank engines and at least one ex Hull & Barnsley Railway 0-6-2 tank were the usual engines to be found in steam on the now rather woebegone weed-grown track which was virtually invisible from the air. Official instructions were given for the line to retain its built-in camouflage when an Ordnance Depot was built near Layerthorpe station in 1942 and the War Department established a petrol store at Murton Lane. The railway had a hectic war with nearby aerodromes at Elvington calling for building materials, then bombs, and the lineside became a vast fuel and explosions dump. It was indeed very fortunate that only two incendiary bombs were recorded as landing during the hostilities. The rundown railway escaped the nationalisation of the four main lines but when British

Railways closed the Selby-Market Weighton line, sealing off the southern outlet of the D.V.L.R., the gradual reduction of the line commenced. First to close was the Wheldrake to Cliff Common section in February, 1963, then back to Elvington in 1968, finally finishing at its present terminus at Dunnington in 1973, giving a total run of 4¼ miles.

Lineside development was to be the key to the railway's future, a mechanical coal plant at Layerthorpe and a grain drying plant at Dunnington being the principal users of the line. With the rundown of British Railways' steam, dieselisation became inevitable, and the first example was a Drewery 204 h.p. 0-6-0 diesel shunter hired in 1961. So successful was this introduction that the company purchased two of these, B.R. Nos. D2298 and D2245, which became D.V.L.R. Nos. 1 and 2. The present chairman of the railway is Roy Cook, managing director of Yorkshire Grain Dryers Ltd., of Dunnington, who set up his business on the line in 1962 and took the chair in 1970. Under his progressive leadership the line has prospered and formally dropped the word 'light' from the company's title on 23rd March, 1973.

No doubt the opening of the now world famous National Railway Museum at York in 1975 gave the spark to the idea of vintage steam trains on the D.V.L.R. as a tourist attraction, and in September, 1976, with full T.V. coverage, the ex London & North Western Railway No. 790 2-4-0 **Hardwicke,** built at Crewe in 1873, hauled the ex-private coach of the Duke of Sutherland for a directors' trial special, following in October by three runs for the general public. Confident that the railway was on to a winner, a regular steam passenger service was re-introduced on 4th May, 1977, for the summer months, one train each afternoon, apart from Mondays, motive power to be **Joem** hauling three ex British Railways coaches repainted in the old company livery. Initially on hire **Joem**, a J72 class 0-6-0T locomotive, was built by British Railways at Darlington in 1951 but its design, nonetheless, dates back to the end of the last century. Purchased for private preservation by R. Ainsworth, who gave it the name **Joem,** it was restored to full N.E.R. livery in 1967 and saw service on the Keighley & Worth Valley Railway for a number of years. Unfortunately the service did not produce the anticipated receipts, and in 1979 it was announced that it would cease at the end of the summer season.**Joem** and three coaches were due to be auctioned in October 1979 in aid of the International Year of the Child.

The Sand Hutton Light Railway

MANY of the early miniature railways were private lines in the estates of country landowners, built in some cases not as purely pleasure lines but in fact as railways of a very narrow gauge. The most notable Yorkshire example of a private line was the one built for Sir Robert Walker on his estate at Sand Hutton Hall, eight miles north of York. Sir Robert was a friend of Arthur Heywood, the exponent of the 15 in gauge concept (or 'minimum gauge' as he preferred it). Heywood carried out his pioneer work on the Duffield Bank railway in Derbyshire and his launch-type boilered locomotives were probably the first attempt at the standardisation of parts over a range of locomotives of tiny narrow gauge designs. With such a contact, it was inevitable that Sir Robert was to settle for 1 ft 3 in as his choice of gauge.

Turning to Bassett-Lowke for his locomotive, he purchased their first 'Class 30' Atlantic and had it named **Synolda** after his wife. The engine was the prototype of a class of three built as the final development of Greenly's 'Little Giant' design of 1904, enlarged and improved over the years to give 30% more traction effort, and sold as being capable of moving up to 90 passengers when advertised in 1911 for the asking price of £380. The Sand Hutton line took delivery of **Synolda** in the summer of 1912 in time for its opening, when it ran from the Sand Hutton village main drive estate entrance for a modest 350 yards, but it was extended by the end of the following year to 1,245 yards.

Sir Robert was intent on the railway reaching the local main line at Warthill station so that it would, in effect, serve the estate rather than be a pure passenger line, but by the outbreak of war in 1914, when the initial target of almost a two mile circuit of the hall had not been achieved, it was destined never to be completed. Nonetheless, the line was very attractive and quite an engineering achievement with some severe grades as steep as 1 in 35 in places and embankments as high as 4 ft near the main 'Garden' station. It included the obligatory tunnel incorporated through a shrubbery for 30 feet, whilst on its run by the lake it had to bridge one of the streams on its way to the terminus at Fishponds.

Despite being a private line, the estate was open on occasion to the public and the railway attracted a lot of local interest, particularly with the younger members of the community. As Ken Hartley recalls in his delightful book on the line, published by the Narrow Gauge Railway Society in 1964:- 'The prospect of a ride on the railway after attending Sunday School was a big inducement to certain youngsters who would, no doubt, otherwise have endeavoured to forego their religious instruction.'

The rolling stock in the early days was four standard Bassett-Lowke four-wheel timber-bodied eight-seater coaches with 5ft wheelbase plus two other vehicles built on the estate, one a bogie saloon coach to seat ten passengers and the other a four-wheel passenger brake van. Details of any freight stock left over from the construction have not survived but some small four-wheel wagons are known to have existed. Many tests were carried out on the line and **Synolda** always gave a good performance. At one time with a load of 8 tons 4 cwts behind the tender, she pounded up grade for 300 yards at 14 m.p.h. Over 20 m.p.h. at times was normal and, given her head, the locomotive was capable of reaching 35 m.p.h., but the numerous curves and changes of grade on the line precluded continuous high speed running with rails only 1 ft 3 in apart.

The railway closed for the duration of the First World War, Sir Robert being a very keen supporter of the Territorials. He was soon posted to New Zealand to assist in training the troops, his wife and estate engineer George L. Batty going with him, George to act as his chauffeur. No doubt the two men who loved their railway talked for hours on the other side of the world about plans for the future when peace eventually came. They both returned to Yorkshire in 1919 and Sir Robert lost no time in drawing up his masterplan to change his miniature railway into a genuine estate line to serve the farms on his land. The project was to connect Warthill station on the York/Market Weighton line of the North Eastern Railway to the village of Scrayingham on the River Derwent via Sand Hutton, plus two branch lines, making a total system of 7¼ miles. An application for a Light Railway Order to the Minister of Transport gained his official approval to the scheme. Work started in May 1920 from Warthill and by the end of the year the line had reached Sand Hutton, and the branch to Claxton was in as far as the brickworks—a great potential source of traffic to the line—a total of three miles of new track. Doubts arose about further expansion when it was realised that scale miniature locomotives were not really suitable for the topography beyond Sand Hutton.

A design was proposed by Greenly for a powerful 2-8-4 locomotive for 15in gauge, which would have been a most impressive machine with a frame length of 17 ft 2 in and a maximum height of 4 ft 9 in. The cylinders proposed were 5¼ in x 8¼ in and the estimated total weight was to be 7,100 lbs. With a working pressure of 125 lbs. per square inch, she was intended to be able to haul on the level 31 tons, with a tractive effort (at 80%) of 1,100 lbs. It was clear, however, that the new railway could not be completed without a re-think of the combination of gauge and suitable motive power without letting the overall cost get out of hand, and plans for any brand new locomotive were soon abandoned.

The Government sale of the locomotives and stock of the Deptford Meat Depot on the Thames came up in December, 1920. It was anticipated that here was a good source of cheap equipment, for after all, the 18 in gauge steam locomotives were hardly run in. Sir Robert made up his mind that his new line must be 18 in gauge and he would purchase three locomotives and wagons at the sale to furnish all that was required for an efficient light railway (but a fourth locomotive was added late in 1927). Two years elapsed in the job of changing the gauge to 1ft 6in and by late 1922 **Synolda** was redundant and up for sale. The travels of this historic locomotive are something of a mystery for a time, but it turned up on the Belle Vue miniature railway at Manchester bearing the name **Prince Charles.** For a time it ran with a very crude external rebuild to try to make it look like an American old-time Western-style locomotive, but the story has a happy ending for now the locomotive has found its way to Ravenglass and after restoration it forms the centrepiece of the new railway museum being assembled at the station.

The Sand Hutton line in its revised form was completed by the end of 1923 and a passenger service on Saturdays and York market days was introduced the following October, after the Government inspector had given his approval. It was, of course, freight that was to be the mainstay of the line—general agricultural products with special regard for sugar beet and potatoes, and the 20,000 bricks a day from the Claxton works, a plant which had no motor road access.

The line started from the Warthill exchange sidings with the L.N.E.R. and ran parallel with the Hull line for about half a mile before following the course of an old bridle path to White Sike junction, the start of the brickworks branch, from where it continued to Sand Hutton Central, a distance of two miles, to Gardens Halt, War Memorial Halt, Kissthorns Halt and finally to the terminus at Bossall station, a total of 4½ miles. The track actually continued to join the Barnby branch, which it was intended would reach Scrayingham, but this required a single-span bridge over the River Derwent, the estimated cost of which was always beyond the resources of the line, and was never built.

All four of the locomotives obtained were of a distinctive 0-4-0 well tank design (water tank between the frames), built by the

Hunslet Engine Co. Ltd., Leeds, in 1917, their Works Nos. being 1207 (the last to be purchased) and 1289/1291. On the Sand Hutton these ran as **Esme** (after Sir Robert's second wife) and 2, 3 and 4 respectively. With tiny 6½in x 8in cylinders and a wheelbase of 3ft 6in, these little gems weighed only 5 tons 19 cwt in full working order. Their only drawback was the limited water tank capacity of 58 gallons, which necessitated frequent water stops to replenish, usually by means of a bucket poured into a funnel through the tank filler pipe situated on the footplate in front of the smokebox door.

The freight stock was all ex Deptford and consisted of a fleet of very solid four-wheel underframes which carried removable drop-sided bodies, the rated load capacity being 2½ tons (or 750 bricks). Four narrow gauge wagons neatly filled one main line 10 ton open wagon. A brake van was purchased new from Robert Hudson's of Leeds in 1923—a rather heavy vehicle with 6ft wheelbase and some 15ft overall length fitted with sliding doors, but it normally worked on the passenger trains. For this service, the line had only one coach, also by Hudson's in 1924. A most handsome 6-ton diamond bogie vehicle, it was 32 ft 9 in long, a giant for 18in gauge. Inside, two compartments incorporated seating for 30 passengers and an extra saloon section had six movable chairs for its patrons, and for a time this doubled up as a buffet car during summer months. In the good old days a service of three passenger trains on Saturdays was worked with 40 minutes allowed for the 4½ miles, a time which was normally greatly reduced to allow plenty of time to make main line connections with York trains, the fare from Bossall to Warthill being 8d single.

The railway over the years began to get a rather woebegone appearance with deteriorating trackwork. By the time of Sir Robert Walker's death in 1930 the writing was on the wall for his beloved line, when at the end of the year the total passenger receipts added up to just £1. Final abandonment came in June, 1932, and the well known railway undertakers, T.W. Ward of Sheffield, came in to dismantle the line, and the tiny Hunslets, which today would be worth a fortune, went under the torch to be reduced to scrap on the site—not even a plate was saved! It is indeed fortunate that the Narrow Gauge Railway Society stepped in and saved a similar locomotive **Jack**, Hunslet No. 684/1898, after it was presented by John Knowles (Wooden Box) Ltd., of Woodville, Leicestershire, and had it moved to Leeds in October, 1958, where it is in store for the long awaited Armley Mill Industrial History Museum.

The unique Hudson coach has had a chequered career. Presumably the underframe went for scrap but the body was purchased after closure by a local farmer for use as a pavilion by the Harton Ladies Cricket Team (Women's Lib came early to Yorkshire), where it was set up on a cinder bed, the windows on the side away from the pitch being blanked off with corrugated iron sheeting. Over the years, inevitably, decay set in but it lasted long enough for the preservation boom and its remains were finally acquired by the Lincolnshire Coast Light Railway and moved to their 2ft gauge line at Humberstone, three miles south of Cleethorpes, in June, 1967. It was then remounted on a chassis created from two ex War Department 60 cm. gauge wagons. The resourcefulness of the preservationists these days knows no bounds—no doubt Sir Robert would have approved.

2. Mainly Industrial Lines

INDUSTRIAL lines and tramways were the first ever railways and the lines that served the collieries of Yorkshire have a very long history. One or two provided a private passenger service or 'Paddy train' as it was usually called for the miners, and probably the best known was the Waterloo Main Colliery line at Temple Newsam, Leeds, where ex-Metropolitan railway carriages were used.

The two lines covered in this section, however, did provide a regular timetable service for the public and are thus worthy of inclusion for that reason alone.

The Aberford Railway

THIS was one railway completely different to all the others covered in this brief survey for, being mainly a private industrial line, it was not subject to an Act of Parliament. By far the earliest line to be covered, it was orginally surveyed for Richard Oliver Gascoigne of Parlington Hall, the local colliery owner, in the early 1830s to cross his estate and serve the Elizabeth and Isabella pits by means of a three mile standard gauge railway connecting the historic coaching town of Aberford to Garforth, 7¼ miles from Leeds. Garforth was on the new Leeds & Selby Railway, the first main line in the area, and a company of which the Gascoigne family were shareholders. Its passenger service started on 22nd September, 1834.

The survey for the Aberford Railway came up with a single line of just about a continuous falling grade to Aberford. No official records of the survey or opening of the line have survived, but wagons probably started rolling during 1835, the coal being handled in the old fashioned chaldron wagons of the day. A passenger service was introduced in 1837, when a primitive four-wheel coach was fashioned in the colliery workshops. This unique vehicle became known as the 'High Flyer' and looked rather like a timber garden shed on wheels with a brakesman's platform at one end and three tiny windows near the roof line on each side, which resulted in a dim interior fitted with bench seats. The brakesman had control of a roof-mounted bell to give notice of the train's approach at the line's ungated crossings. The normal method of operation was for the coach to be connected to the horse or pony providing the motive power for uphill working ahead of the string of coal wagons; bringing up the rear of the train was a horse Dandy car. The horse had to be well trained for at the start of a downhill section it was unhitched on the move and, as the train passed on its freewheeling way, it had to jump smartly on to the car.

As if all this was not complicated enough, on the incline between Isabella and Sisters pits the trains were hauled up by a stationary steam engine. On wet days in the woods, if the horse could not gain a sure footing, it was common practice for the passengers to have to put a shoulder to the train! The initial passenger service was short-lived as a local horse-bus service started up in competition between Aberford and Leeds on market days after the 'Railway King', George Hudson, closed the Leeds & Selby line to passengers for a time. The 'Fly Line', as it became known, reinstated its gravity passenger service in 1850 on a regular market day basis on Tuesdays and Saturdays, and its connection with the main line was improved in 1852. If contemporary accounts are anything to go by it was not before time as, prior to the improvements, passengers at Garforth had to make use of the station master's bedroom as a waiting room and tickets were issued via the kitchen window. As an indication of the volume of traffic being handled, a new siding was laid out at Garforth in 1865 to accommodate up to 60 wagons and it was soon evident that steam traction would have to be introduced.

The first locomotive **Mulciber**, a Manning Wardle product to their Works No. 319, was supplied in 1870, soon to be followed by **Ignifer** from the same builders in 1871. Both were of the Boyne Engine Works class 'H' design of 0-4-0 saddle tank with 12ins x 18ins outside cylinders and driving wheels 3ft 0ins in diameter. The third Manning locomotive, No. 1254, arrived in 1897. Named **Empress** to honour the Queen's Diamond Jubilee, it was an enlarged version of the first engine and was designated Class I by the builders and incorporated 13ins x 18ins outside cylinders. The introduction of steam did not put the 'High Flyer' out of its free-wheeling business as it was intended that steam would only be used against the grade to Garforth.

By 1887, the Aberford residents petitioned for a return of a daily passenger service and Colonel Gascoigne, then in charge of the Garforth Collieries, after first checking that he would not be breaking the law, introduced a service on six days a week. As the old 'High Flyer' was nearing the end of its days, he purchased an aged secondhand, teak-finished four-wheeled coach probably of Midland Railway origin, with four compartments, one 1st class upholstered in blue and three 3rd class finished in red. The fare structure remained at 3d single and 6d return 3rd class, with the new 1st class standing at 9d return. To avoid any problems with the line's status, when introduced the card tickets carried the warning on the reverse side:-

> 'The owners of Garforth Colliery, who convey passengers on their private railway, do so for the accommodation of the public, and will not be responsible for any injury, loss, damage or casualty, from whatever cause the same may occur.'

Despite this reminder that the line was a private industrial one, it had a remarkable safety record, apart from odd derailments. In fact the only casualty recalled was the first horse that worked the train, which reputedly ended its life by falling down a coal chute at Aberford. Because of the nature of the railway, the timetable was a rather leisurely affair with a nominal time of 15 minutes being allowed for the three mile run, and an official speed limit of 12 m.p.h. was imposed. The journey through the fields and woods was something of a delightful excursion in the old days, particularly in early spring, and the scenes in the snows of winter when the deer in Parlington Park ran away from the steam trains would have had present-day camera-toting railway enthusiasts shooting off reels of colour film.

The Gascoigne family sold out its colliery interests in 1920, and the new company, Garforth Collieries Ltd., undertook to retain the railway and maintain a public service, but Sisters Pit closed in 1922 to be followed by Isabella in 1925, both completely worked out. The inevitable final nail in the coffin came with the introduction of a local motor bus service in December 1920, and the line soon reverted to market day passenger trains only, the final one steaming into the records books in March 1924 after some 87 years of unconventional service to the commuter.

A new pit opened at Barnbow in 1925 but the Garforth company had a hard time of it after the General Strike of 1926 and finally went into bankruptcy in 1930. As regards the fate of the locomotives, **Mulciber** had left the line by 1912 for service at Low Laithes Colliery near Wakefield. After the closure of the company, **Empress** finished up at Old Silkstone and poor **Ignifer** had a long drawn out end—the frames complete with boiler were left in the old 'Fly Shed' at Hawks Nest and, over the years, the elements with assistance from vandals reduced the remains of the locomotive and shed to scrap. The line's single coach fared somewhat better being converted into a local bungalow.

Little remains of the line today. The Garforth end has altered out of all recognition, and what was once a colliery village is now modern suburbia and a dormitory area for Leeds. Aberford has been by-passed by the Great North Road, but even with some new property it has retained its old world character and the remains of the railway yard and stables can still be discerned just off the main street.

The East and West Yorkshire Union Railway

DESPITE its impressive title, the East and West Yorkshire Union Railway was never much more than a standard gauge colliery line. In fact, it only qualifies for inclusion in this survey on account of its very brief venture into the passenger business, which was nothing less than a total disaster.

None the less it was an interesting system, the origins of which date back to ambitious proposals as early as 1881 when a group of colliery owners and other parties interested in the development of the West Yorkshire coalfield came up with plans for a 30 mile line. The basic concept was for a standard gauge railway to connect Ardsley, on the Great Northern Railway, with Drax, on the line then under construction for the Hull, Barnsley & West Riding Junction Railway, and it promised to provide an alternative route between Leeds and the West Riding and Hull. It is not surprising that the North Eastern Railway was less than enthusiastic about the idea, losing no time in putting up a lot of opposition, and in the end, the Bill failed to get the approval of the House of Lords.

The Upper House relented at the second attempt with a revised Bill two years later and the powerful Joseph Charlesworth, J.P., at the head of the East & West Yorkshire Union Board issued a prospectus in October 1887 to raise capital for the venture. Charlesworth was the chairman of the J. & J. Charlesworth Colliery Co., and as such had most to gain from the proposed railway, but the extensive main line was not to be. Funds were not forthcoming and the eventual railway which came into being was a little over nine miles in length.

Due to the hilly nature of the land to the south of Leeds, the line was not easy to build for the contractors, Whittaker Bros. of Horsforth, and involved extensive earthworks and deep cuttings. The first section opened for freight traffic on 20th May, 1891, but to be of any practical use an outlet to Leeds was essential. A nominally independent company entitled the South Leeds Junction Railway, with a line from Rothwell to Stourton, opened in 1895, being operated by Charlesworth and acquired by the East and West Yorkshire Union from July of the same year.

The completed system consisted of a double track main line between Stourton and Lofthouse, via Rothwell and Robin Hood. Stourton Junction formed a facing connection with the Midland Railway's line between Hunslet and Woodlesford and, at the Lofthouse end, Lofthouse Colliery Junction made a trailing connection with the Great Northern Railway. Three single track branches added the finishing touches. The most important was the Newmarket line from Robin Hood, two miles 55 chains in length, serving the prosperous Newmarket Collieries. The other two short lines, each some ¾ mile in length, served Beeston Colliery, and the Thorpe on the Hill branch hauled stone traffic from the quarries as well as the produce of the Robin Hood Collieries. For many years the railway was renowned for its excellent trackwork, which incorporated 95lb. bull-head rail, the maximum permitted speed limit being set at 15 m.p.h. for coal and freight working.

The original intention of the promoters was to provide a passenger service but in the line's reduced form they could hardly have been enthusiastic about starting one. Their market research in the end could not have been carried out with any degree of efficiency, for what was eventually provided lasted a mere nine months and was a giant millstone round the railway's neck. The service hardly got off to a good start for the inaugural train departed from the Midland Railway's Wellington Street station in Leeds bound for Rothwell on 4th January, 1904, when the whole area was shrouded in thick fog. The official party, headed by the new chairman, C. E. Charlesworth, had lunch in Rothwell station booking hall, followed by the usual toasting and speech making. The announcement that directors and officials of the line should have permanent free passes gave the service an air of solidity.

The regular five trains a day in each direction between Leeds and Robin Hood, stopping at Hunslet, Stourton and Rothwell, were augmented with an extra one on Tuesdays and Saturdays, but reduced to three trains each way on Sundays. By August, the Sunday service was withdrawn and the writing was on the wall for the whole service, which finally closed on 30th September, 1904—nine months from optimism to total despair! It had hardly time to find its way into the railway timetable, where, incidentally, it was listed under the title of The Rothwell Railway (Leeds to Rothwell and Robin Hood) and the full run was allowed twenty minutes—five to Hunslet, ten to Stourton, seventeen to Rothwell and twenty to Robin Hood. The passenger rolling stock and the motive power for working the trains was provided on hire by the Midland Railway, a continuous and expensive drain on the slim resources of the small railway. Two locomotives were provided by the main line company, both Johnson 0-4-4 tanks, No. 6 (later 1226) and 1265, and the coaches although not recorded were almost certainly of the six-wheel variety.

The downfall of the passenger system can mainly be attributed to the spread of the local tramway network. The Yorkshire (West Riding) Electric Tramways and Leeds Corporation opened up between Leeds and Rothwell and Leeds and Wakefield via Robin Hood in 1904/5. The directors must have known about the forthcoming tram invasion which had been on the way for over two years, but still they tried in vain to compete.

The line then settled down to its main claim to fame which was its efficient freight-handling capacity with a fleet of over 300 wagons. Over the years, passenger trains did traverse the lines to Rothwell, starting with occasional Great Northern Railway excursion trains, usually bound for Bridlington or Cleethorpes, in which case they had to traverse the section of main line not previously covered by the regular passenger service.

With the 1923 railway amalgamation and the formation of the big four, the East & West Yorkshire Union lost its identity and became a minor part of the London & North Eastern Railway and lasted there until the creation of British Railways. By this time the odd excursion was worked out in the Leeds direction for Blackpool, via Stourton. The final closure came on 3rd October, 1966. By then the Thorpe branch had been cut by the route of the M1 motorway, and soon after the actual dismantling got under way in February 1978 very little was to remain of this interesting old system.

Over the years, many noteworthy locomotives have seen service on coal trains. A lot of these were Charlesworth's colliery shunters which served sidings and spurs to the various parts of the family empire. Whittakers, the Horsforth contractors responsible for the line's construction, made use of the older existing locomotives, notable among which was a superb early Manning Wardle Class I 0-6-0 saddle tank dating back to 1861, which carried the name **Henrietta** and was supplied new on 21st January, 1861, to J. & J. Charlesworth Ltd., Rothwell Haigh for service at their Beeston Colliery. After completion of the East and West Yorkshire Union Railway, it became part of the railway stock for a short period before passing into the hands of Meakin & Dean, Birkenhead. It eventually ended its days on the Hundred of Manhood & Selsey Railway, later called the West Sussex Light Railway, where it ran

Aberford Railway—1. Empress heads a 1920s' estate workers and family special towards Garforth. (Author's collection)

Manning Wardle Empress blows off as it pauses at the Light Arch, circa 1921. (Author's collection)

MULCIBER

Above: The Waterloo Main Colliery 'paddy train' in 1954 with Hudswell 0-4-0 ST Kitchener built in 1914. The timber carried on the leading buffer beam had been used for re-railing packings just prior to the photograph. (R. N. Redman)

Opposite: Aberford Railway—2.

Top: The classic Manning Wardle 0-4-0 ST as typified by the Aberford Railway's first locomotive Mulciber, Works No. 319 of 1870. (Author's collection)

Bottom: The famous High Flyer. Note the heavy wooden brake blocks, essential for a coach that freewheeled down the line's three mile grade. (Author's collection)

East & West Yorkshire Union Railway—1. Builder's photograph of No. 2, by Manning Wardle & Co. to their Works No. 1308 in 1895. (Author's collection)

Manning Wardle & Co.'s official photograph of No. 4, prior to departure from the Boyne Engine Works in 1898. (Author's collection)

East & West Yorkshire Union Railway—2. No. 5, built by Manning Wardle & Co. in 1899. (Real Photographs Co. Ltd)

No. 5 in its short lived guise as LNER No. 3115. Photographed at Ardsley shed prior to withdrawal in 1928. (Real Photographs Co. Ltd.)

Shipley Glen Tramway. Sold for many years, this attractive commercial card purchased in 1958 shows well the delightful wooded setting of the tramway and the very light and rather uneven trackwork. (Author's collection)

The lower station of the tramway. The train on the left is one of the originals dating back to 1895. Photographed circa 1950. (E. G. Cope)

Spurn and Kilnsea Railway—1. Lifeboatmen's sail powered bogie in service at Spurn Point. (K. E. Hartley collection)

The vintage Vulcan Foundry locomotive Kenyon in its final form running as a 2-2-2- saddle tank. (K. E. Hartley collection)

Spurn and Kilnsea Railway—2.
Above: Builder's official photograph of the Hudswell Clarke petrol railcar built in 1933. (Author's collection)

Opposite, top: Spurn Point train in steam days with Kenyon in its 'middle period' running as a 2-4-0 saddle tank. (Courtesy N. Redmayne/K.E. Hartley)

Opposite, bottom: A light railway 'special'. The Itala racing car converted to run on the Spurn Point line. (J. Codd, K. E. Hartley collection)

S.V.M.R.

Above: North Bay Railway, Scarborough: Northstead Manor Gardens' star attractions in the early 1930s. The North Bay Railway's second Pacific Triton heads a full train along the edge of the boating lake just as the water chute drenches another load of delighted holidaymakers. (Author's collection)

Opposite: Sunnyvale Pleasure Gardens Railway

Top: The railway as recorded by this vintage commercial postcard—Yorkshire cloth caps well to the fore. (K. E. Hartley)

Bottom: The 15'' gauge railway in 1923—Bassett-Lowke Atlantic Baby Bunce. (K. E. Hartley)

The "Elizabeth", Saltburn Miniature Railway.

Pickering
Z.1

Above: Golden Acre Park Miniature Railway—1. May Thompson about to depart from Lakeside station with a loaded train in the late 1930s. (Collection E. G. Cope)

Opposite, top: Rio Grande Express, Garforth. Train standing in the Cactus Junction station of Yorkshire's latest miniature railway at Saville Brothers, Garforth Garden Centre. (I. Stephenson)

Opposite, bottom: Saltburn Miniature Railway. 15 in gauge petrol engined 4-4-4 tank Elizabeth on a light train. The lack of a smokebox door is due to this being a grill to allow air flow to the front mounted radiator. (Author's collection)

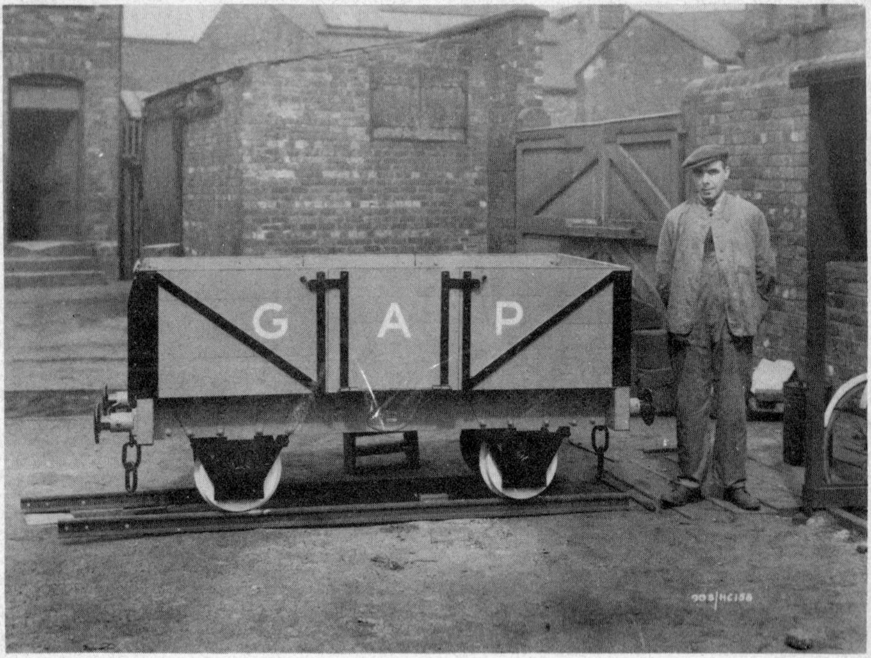

Golden Acre Park Miniature Railway—2.

Above: Scale freight rolling stock is rather rare. This is one of a set of open wagons built by Hudswell Clarke & Co. Ltd., for the Golden Acre Park railway. Photographed in the works yard with fitter Harry Fields standing by to show the scale. (Author's collection)

Opposite, top: Baltic tank locomotive Robin Hood. Photographed at the Railway Foundry, Leeds, in 1932 prior to delivery. (Author's collection)

Opposite, bottom: Lightweight inspection car powered by a 300 c.c. J.A.P. engine with a belt drive to the rear axle. It must have had a fair turn of speed when built in 1933 by Hudswell Clarke & Co. Ltd. for the sum of £85.00. (Author's collection)

ROBIN HOOD
1932
H.C99

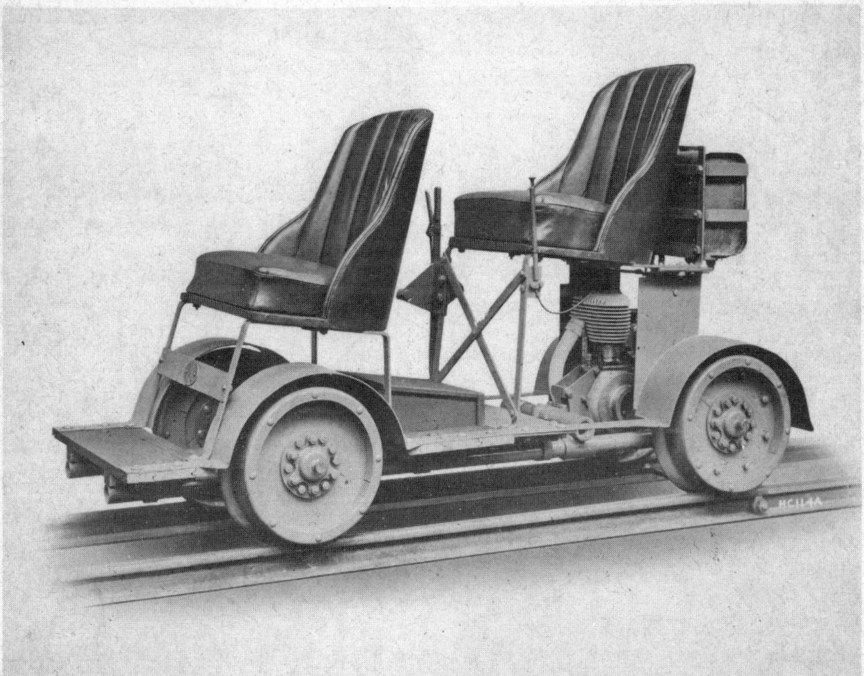
HC114A

Newby Hall Miniature Railway. Yorkshire's finest miniature railway steam locomotive, the Newby Hall 10¼in gauge Royal Scot in September, 1978. (R. N. Redman)

Royal Scot with a full head of steam being manhandled round on the turntable at the line's terminus, September, 1978. (R. N. Redman)

for many years, renamed **Sidlesham.** This line finally closed during January, 1935.

For the first five years' operation of the E. & W.Y.U., apart from industrial locomotives, some of the line's traffic was entrusted to Great Northern Railway engines, but in 1895 the first new motive power was delivered from the nearby Manning Wardle's Boyne Engine Works. These carried road Nos. 1 and 2, and Works Nos. 1307/8; both were 0-6-0 saddle tanks with 17 ins x 24 ins inside cylinders driving 4 ft diameter wheels and had a working order weight of 39 tons 12 cwt. After absorption by the L.N.E.R., they were classified as Class J84 and became Nos. 3112 and 3113, the former being withdrawn in 1930 and the latter in 1928.

A smaller Manning Wardle 0-6-0 saddle tank became the line's first No. 3, built in 1895 to maker's No. 1325. Its 15 ins x 20 ins cylinders may have been a little underpowered, for it was soon re-sold in 1899 to Wath Main Colliery where it became their No. 7. A duplicate of the first two engines became the new No. 3, built as Manning Wardle No. 1489 of 1900; she finished up in L.N.E.R. hands but was not renumbered and was scrapped after takeover in 1923.

In 1898, the original basic 0-6-0 design was extended to an 0-6-2 saddle tank and the line's No. 4 took this form as Manning Wardle No. 1398. It later returned to the makers in 1919 and emerged after extensive re-building as an 0-6-0 saddle tank. The 0-6-2 saddle tank format was retained for Nos. 5 and 6, built by Manning Wardle in 1899 to their Nos. 1433 and 1434. These were not rebuilt and finished up as L.N.E.R. Class N19. No. 5 became L.N.E.R. 3115 and was finally withdrawn in 1928, but No. 6 was not renumbered and was withdrawn on takeover in 1923.

After the L.N.E.R. moved in, the locomotives retained were transferred to Ardsley. No doubt some of the fitters on shed were familiar with the Mannings for they had carried out repairs over the years for the independent line, but for major work the locomotives had returned to Jack Lane in Hunslet and, like the Charlesworth engines, came back to the builders under their own steam. As the older locomotives were phased out their place was taken by main line motive power, the most popular being the six-coupled side and saddle tanks allocated to Ardsley shed.

3. The Odd Ones Out

THIS is the section for the two lines that will not fit in under the other general headings. The Shipley Glen Tramway is the only cable-worked line included. Consideration was given to the standard gauge cliff-lift tramways at Scarborough, all still running and providing an efficient service in this hilly resort, but with runs of under 300 feet they were excluded.

The Spurn and Kilnsea Railway was War Department property, but certainly had over it some of the most unusual forms of motive power ever to run on rails. Can any other line boast sail power and a rebuilt racing car, as well as steam and internal combustion railcars?

The Shipley Glen Tramway

THIS tiny 20-inch gauge cable worked funicular, hidden away on a woodland hillside near Baildon, is a delightful piece of Victoriana that is happily still with us and forms one of the least-known of our minor passenger railways.

The Glen and Walker Woods were first developed by Colonel Maude, Lord of the Manor of Baildon, towards the end of the last century. It did not take long for the area's abundance of fresh air to attract crowds who came at weekends by train and tram to escape for a few hours from their grimy mill environment. The good picnic areas and play space for children made it a major attraction in those peaceful pre-family car days, especially at bluebell time.

During the 1890s it became obvious that the steep paths of the

Glen were hard work for the very young or elderly visitors and a cable-worked incline was proposed by Samuel Wilson, a local man who was a pioneer in the provision of amusements. One of his claims to fame was the operation of Shipley's first cinema-cum-variety show and a good indication of his flamboyant character can be gained from his recollections at his 80th birthday of his younger days, when he once smoked a cigar and drank a glass of beer in the lion's cage during an actual performance without a tremor! Wilson first had ideas about building his own railway to the top of the moors in line with Victoria Road, Saltaire, but could not get consent from all the intervening landowners and thus hit on the idea of more or less following a path through Walker Woods to the Glen. He proposed this alternative route to landowner Colonel Maude, who liked the idea and when Sam asked him about a rent he received the reply 'What do you say to giving me £10 a year?'

The first problem was a supply of gas to power the winding engine and Wilson lost no time in contacting Sir James Roberts to try and connect into the pipes which supplied Saltaire Mills. Sir James agreed but had doubts about the wisdom of a tramway up the hillside. When he asked Sam Wilson, he got the characteristic reply, 'I am building it for seven reasons, for the old and the young, for the lame and the lazy, for the weak and the strong, and lastly for myself.'

Work started by clearing the right of way of about 30 trees and removing a large number of rocks, and the laying of 600 yards of gas pipe from the coach road. A lot of this work was personally carried out by Wilson, possibly assisted by a partner in the venture, a Mr. H. Wilkinson. They had hopes of opening the new line on Good Friday, 1895, but it was a terrible winter that year with ice in the area up to 18 inches thick.

At last the tramway was finished and opened for business the day after the official inspection on Friday, 17th May, 1895. It was a twin track incline only 600 yards in length - but what it lacked in length of run it made up for in climbing grades as steep as 1 in 12. The odd gauge of 20 inches has been the source of much speculation over the years, and it has been suggested that the two main men connected with the project had gained some experience of a similar gauged system in France. However, Wilson, on at least one interview with the local press, stated that he travelled all over the country to examine lines which had been successfully established and that it was on the little railway at Aberystwyth that the Glen tramway was based.

From its inception it was intended to be very much a local product. Sam Halliday & Sons of Baildon supplied the first two pairs of 12-seater passenger cars, unique in having their bodies raised at one end to compensate for the effect of the steep gradient. A Mr. Robson of Shipley delivered the 8 h.p. gas engine along with its 4ft 6ins diameter gear to drive the cable drum. The cable itself was 5/8 ins in diameter with a breaking strain of 14½ tons and was wrapped 1¾ times around the 6ft 6ins diameter drum to avoid any chance of slipping. Estimates of the total cost of building the line varied from an initial low of £500 to about £1,000, but Wilson recalled later that it had set him back £2,500.

Whatever the cost, it was an immediate success, and soon settled down to an uneventful existence with pairs of 14ft long passenger cars rolling up and down at an average speed of 15 m.p.h., with passengers out of pocket to the tune of a penny for the journey up and a halfpenny to come down. One of its less pleasant duties was to carry coffins and funeral parties down to carriages waiting at the foot of the Glen.

When Sam Wilson retired in 1919, it was estimated that the line had carried 7,500,000 passengers without mishap, still using all the original equipment! In 1928, twin 35 h.p. electric motors replaced the gas engine, but the passenger stock was not renewed until after the 1955 summer season. Webb's Truck Co. of Bradford supplied the new stock which in true Yorkshire tradition incorporated a number of parts from the original 1895 vehicles. The new cars were finished in a green livery, the end panels of which were repainted red with a five pointed star motif in 1957, and for the following five years the trains carried the names of the royal children, the eastern coach named **Charles** and the western one called **Anne.** The line normally ran daily from Easter to September with additional weekend working 'if the weather looked promising' in March or October, and in the good old days as many as 17,000 people have been carried in a single day.

Several proprietors have worked the tramway this century, among them J.E. Woodhead who even ran a 'scholars' service with fares of a halfpenny for either direction. H. Parr of Baildon took control during 1931, and Glen Tramways Ltd., as the line had become, changed hands in 1943. The new concern carried on until 1966, by which time the railway was becoming very 'down at heel' and had its first accident when a car over-ran the platform, so the company called a halt, no doubt to avoid the crippling cost of re-furbishing the whole line. Inevitably in these days, vandals moved in on the moribund remains to speed up the effects of nature, but all was not lost. Glen Enterprises Ltd. took over the remains in late 1968 and lost no time in restoring the line and reinstating a weekend service, starting 12th June, 1969. Now it is again possible to ride through the woods on the narrow gauge as our grandparents did, but at current rates of 8p single and 16p return for adults, with children under five costing 6p single or 12p return.

Samuel Wilson died aged 83 in January 1940. His little tramway lives on, but it was not the only tracked attraction he built in the area at the turn of the century. No date can be traced for the construction of the other ride—'The Toboggan Slide'—but it must have been during the late 1890s (possibly in association with another Shipley cinema pioneer, John Sagar, who was also in business as an ironmonger, and who was definitely connected with a lot of his friend Sam's innovations). An all timber runway carried a multi-wooden track railway down the steep Baildon side of the Glen and part way up the other side to reduce the speed of the free-running toboggans before they reached the buffer stops at the end of the run. Once the toboggans accumulated at the end of the runs, provision was made for a cable-hauled car to draw them to the top of the slope.

It is not surprising that this ride was recalled as 'exciting and breathless and terrifically fast', if one had the courage to try it. Its fame and popularity grew in leaps and bounds until Whit Tuesday, 1900, when an accident occurred at about 7.30 p.m. 'Little Sam', son of the builder, went down the slope with a friend whose hat blew off just after the start. In order to retrieve the hat about 50 yards from the top, 'Little Sam' rode the hauling car back, stopped to collect the head piece, and restarted when possibly a splice on the haulage rope failed and the car raced back out of control. The owner's son was lucky to escape with nothing worse than a broken collar bone. Sam Senior swore he would never work the slide again, and what was without doubt a little goldmine was reduced to vast quantities of timber which were re-sold. No trace of this old time 'thriller' remains.

The Spurn and Kilnsea Railway

THE most isolated of Yorkshire's minor railways was without doubt the 3¾ mile long standard gauge Spurn Head Railway, which connected the village of Kilnsea to Spurn Point at the end of the narrow peninsula of sand and shingle that forms the south-east tip of the county.

The line was not visited by many enthusiasts or would-be passengers, due to the fact that it was owned by the War Department, its origins dating back to the construction of defences to guard the approaches to Hull during the 1st World War. These defences took the form of high-powered guns and searchlights at Spurn and Godwin (Kilnsea) as well as two man-made island forts named Bull Sand and Haile Sand. The contract to carry out all this civil engineering work, as well as 300 yards of sea wall near Kilnsea, was awarded in 1915 to the Manchester contractors, C. J. Wills, experts on railway and dock work. At this time the Point had not even a road over its desolate dunes, the lifeboat station—incidentally, the only station in England to have a full-time crew—being served by sea.

A railway was the obvious choice for moving the prodigious amount of materials required and secondhand main line rail and chairs were used in the construction. C. J. Wills had five steam locomotives on the line, all small contractors' type saddle tanks, three of which were 0-4-0 machines by Hudswell Clarke & Co. Ltd. —**Frances** Works No. 435 of 1895, **Somerton** No. 656 of 1903, and the famous **Lord Mayor** No. 402 of 1893 which worked all over the country on a variety of jobs and contracts before finishing up with George Cohen Sons & Co. Ltd. at their Stanningley, Leeds, depot in 1958. In 1967 it was presented for preservation and is now in full working order on the Keighley & Worth Valley Railway at Haworth. The other two locomotives were both 0-6-0 saddle tanks, **Bombay** by Manning Wardle, No. 1674 of 1906, and the line's long serving veteran locomotive **Kenyon,** built by the Vulcan Foundry Co. Ltd. in 1888 to their Works No. 1233. This last only weighed just over 17 tons empty and was fitted with 12ins x 17ins inside cylinders and was unusual in having solid disc type driving wheels of 3ft diameter. It was used originally on the construction of the Manchester Ship Canal but on completion of the Spurn Defence Contract it was transferred to the War Department to become the line's main locomotive. It was old to start with, and one must assume that all the wind blown sand would cause excessive wear on all the bearings, which was probably the reason for the removal of the leading sections of coupling rods to form a 2-4-0. Eventually the rear section bushes were so worn that the trailing rods were also removed, making **Kenyon** into a 2-2-2. Just about completely worn out, it was finally scrapped in 1929. The only other steam power to see service on Spurn Point was a tiny 0-4-0 tank, L.N.E.R. No. 559 of Class Y8, built in 1890. It came from Hull Dairycoates shed early in 1940 and acquired the nickname 'The Black Sapper' during a stay of about 12 months; it eventually finished up as shed pilot at York before final withdrawal in November, 1949.

When **Kenyon** was not in regular use with its equally antique, four-wheel, five-compartment coach of unknown parentage, the line was given over to very different forms of traction. Two four-wheel sail bogies were introduced, one by the lifeboat men in 1915 and the other by the War Department personnel. These were popular and obviously cheap to run—with a good breeze behind, speeds of 40 m.p.h. have been talked of. In competition with steam or sail, a Royal Engineers officer, Lt. Lee, enjoyed himself with a converted two seater pre-war 'Itala' racing car adapted to run on rails during 1918. The owner used it for a year before moving on but he left his creation behind for future generations of officers to enjoy.

Three forms of passenger railcars worked over the Spurn metals, starting with a 20 h.p. Drewry Car Company 12-seat, petrol-engined, two-ton inspection car in January 1920, and followed by two other smaller versions from the same builder. Four Wheel Drive Motors Ltd. of Slough supplied a 55 h.p. 12-seater vehicle about 1929, which lasted until after the 2nd World War, but was not so popular with the staff as the last railcar, a 30 h.p. 'one-off' design built by Hudswell Clarke & Co. Ltd., Works No. P.265, specifically for the Spurn and Kilnsea line to an order by the Director of Army Contracts. The 20-seat body was subcontracted to Charles Roe & Co. Ltd., the Leeds coach builders, but the final erection was by Hudswells, the overall dimensions being 25 ft long on a 10 ft wheelbase and a maximum width of 9 ft. It was delivered to Spurn on 3rd August, 1933, by chargehand fitter Arthur Kinsey, who soon had it in service. It was to become a popular vehicle on the line and performed manfully for 18 years, seeing a lot of round the clock running during the last war. Even at the end of the line in 1951 it was still doing five workmen's round trip runs per day, and did in fact escape the scrappers' torch by being transferred by road to the Bicester Royal Engineers' Depot in Oxfordshire. It was then stripped down and its chassis converted into a crane runner truck, where it was photographed as recently as 1974. After closure in 1951, Thos. W. Ward Ltd. of Sheffield moved in to carry out their usual thorough job of demolition and very few traces of the line can now be found.

4. Miniature Railways

THOUGH not strictly within the title light railways, the interest in miniature railways has grown over the years. The concept of carrying passengers for pleasure on very narrow gauge track has a long history, and many interesting 'tiny' railways have flourished in Yorkshire, and no doubt more will appear in the years to come. The following are intended to form an introduction into the fascinating sideline of railway history.

The Halifax Zoo Railway

(15 ins gauge)

PROBABLY the two most famous names connected with the development of miniature railways and locomotives are the designer Henry Greenly (1876-1947) and the engineer Wenman Joseph Bassett-Lowke (1877-1953). Their first masterpiece was a 15 ins gauge, 1 ton 9 cwt. 4-4-2 locomotive, a little over a quarter full size design, based on the famous Great Northern Railway Atlantic class. Built over the years 1904/5, the prototype carried the name **Little Giant** on completion and was despatched from the Northampton Works for trials on the private estate line of the Duke of Westminster at Eaton Hall in Cheshire.

Its first revenue earning work was performed on a short line at the South Shore, Blackpool, but the heavy wear on bearings and motion due to the wind-blown sand made the line short-lived and the locomotive, after two years, was refurbished and moved to the new Halifax Zoo line where, after being renamed **Little Elephant**, it ran in immaculate green livery, with plenty of polished brass-work, up to the year 1913. The zoo, situated at the top of Exley

Hill between Halifax and Elland, was for many years a popular local attraction. Apart from the animal collection, it also boasted a permanent amusement park. The new miniature railway was laid out to encircle a major part of the grounds and included the usual artificial tunnel, then an essential fixture on all miniature lines of the period. The coaches were typical Bassett-Lowke products, robust bogie vehicles with five seats to carry ten passengers.

Probably the high point for the zoo and its line came in 1910 when pioneer aviator Grahame White made a three day appearance on the 10th, 11th and 13th June with his Farman biplane for the then colossal sum of £1,000. McKill, the zoo's managing director, with this gamble attracted 10,000 people on the Saturday, and a further 40,000 who gathered in the outlying fields for a free view, thus avoiding the one shilling per head entrance fee. Despite such high points the zoo started to decline, and in 1913 the line closed and the equipment passed into the hands of the Bunce family, who were developing another attraction, the Sunnyvale Pleasure Gardens.

The Sunnyvale Pleasure Gardens Railway

(15 ins gauge)

THIS project by the Bunce family started during the latter years of the Halifax Zoo, but despite acquiring this railway it was a long time before the line was officially opened in the spring of 1923. The locomotive was the prototype **Little Giant**, once again rebuilt. This time its new name on the splashers was **Baby Bunce**, and its tender had been converted to an eight-wheel bogie, rather than the original six-wheel pattern, but the original livery of green with black and white lining was retained. The line was not an ambitious affair, being basically about 300 yards long end to end, laid out beside a long boating lake and near the roller-skating rink. Passenger stock consisted of three old 12-seater coaches painted up in a green and cream livery.

The line lasted until the park closed in 1939 but its famous locomotive was discovered derelict at South Shields in 1964, and purchased by Mr. T.E. Tate, who, with friends, restored it back to its original glory on a half mile line in the grounds of Haswell Lodge, County Durham, opened in 1971 but since closed when the owner moved south.

The North Bay Railway, Scarborough

(20 ins gauge)

THE spread of the railway network changed Scarborough, 'the Queen of the Yorkshire watering places', from a select resort to one for the masses when the lines reached the coast in 1845. Since then, Scarborough has never looked back and it was inevitable that its progressive Corporation should want to build a miniature railway as an attraction. It is perhaps ironic that the line was a product of the slump period as part of a scheme to provide work. It remains to this day one of the best engineered and finest miniature railways in the country with a total run of just over a mile.

The general layout was the work of H.W. Smith, the Borough Engineer from 1896-1933, and was but one part of the extensive development of Northstead Manor Gardens. Prior to construction, tenders were invited from many of the well known miniature locomotive builders, including Bassett-Lowke, who put forward 15 ins gauge with a 3 ins to the foot scale locomotive. Baguley Engineers Ltd., of Burton-on-Trent, favoured a gauge of 20 ins with designs for steam and diesel (steam outline) locomotive, but the final quote and design accepted was from Hudswell Clarke & Co. Ltd. of Leeds, for a one-third scale outline 10¼ ton model of the famous L.N.E.R. A3 Class Pacific but to be powered by a 26 h.p. diesel engine. It was, however, the final drive that was to be the real innovation, which was via a Vickers-Coates torque converter, thus making it when built to Works No. D565 of 1931 and named **Neptune**, the first locomotive in the world to incorporate this form of transmission, later to prove very popular in recent years in modern industrial shunting locomotives. The line was actually built by the Corporation, all the track parts being supplied by Robert Hudson Ltd., and a 2 ft 0 ins gauge 25 h.p. tractor-type locomotive was loaned by Hudswell's for the construction.

Neptune arrived on site three weeks prior to the official opening of the line by the Lord Mayor on the 23rd May, 1931, and the line settled down to hauling trains of 100 passengers in five bogie coaches at speeds of up to 20 m.p.h. through the gardens alongside the boating lake and down the coast to Scalby Mills. In this probably lies the success of the line, as it goes somewhere rather than just round in a circle for an amusement ride. At the end of the first season, the one locomotive had hauled no less than 410,000 passengers, and the line had taken £12,307 in 3d and 6d fares. Another locomotive was essential and an order was placed for Works No. D573 **Triton,** which Hudswells delivered on the 29th April, 1932, identical to **Neptune** and finished in full L.N.E.R. colours apart from the letters 'N.B.R.' on the eight-wheel tender sides, the running numbers on the cab sides being the year built.

A deputation from the Free Church Council tried to stop Sunday running in June 1931, but were over-ruled by the Town Council. The line has run for seven days a week ever since, in the season, and remains substantially as built, apart from a new track layout at the new Scalby Mills station installed at a cost of £18,500. The reverse loop at that end was in a tunnel up to 1962. The line is single track except for a passing loop at Beach station, essential when both locomotives are in service which is normal practice throughout the busy holiday season.

Golden Acre Park Miniature Railway

(20 ins gauge)

A SUPERB LINE, sadly no longer with us, was this attraction, laid out in the 1930s for Frank T. Thompson, the owner of the Golden Acre Park Estate, beside the Otley Road, near Bramhope, and at that time just outside the city boundary. The design of the line was the work of consulting engineer, D.H. Moore, fresh from his success at the Scarborough North Bay railway, and once again Hudswell Clarke and Hudsons supplied the locomotives and tracks. The first motive power was a 20 h.p. steam outline freelance 4-6-4 Baltic tank, weighing eight tons in full working order. It carried the name **Robin Hood** and Works No. D570 of 1932, and came complete with a set of coaches similar to the North Bay pattern, all arriving in good time for the grand opening of the railway by Anna Neagle on Good Friday, 1932.

The line, in its opening year, was merely a straight run from near the main gate, alongside the boating lake, but extension was inevitable as the park started to become a massive attraction. At weekends coaches poured in from far and wide to disgorge vast crowds, and over 30,000 visitors a day was not uncommon— at 2d each entrance fee this meant the only real problem was handling the weight of copper coins which had to be removed in sandbags.

Thompson was nothing if not a showman, with his private speedboat which caused havoc among the rowing boats, and for a time he had on show the famous Schneider Trophy winning Vickers—Supermarine seaplane, the design of which was later to be developed into the immortal 'Spitfire'. But the railway was his pride and joy and he soon wanted it to encircle the lake to give a good 6d ride, rather than the brief 2d straight run, the new line to be carried over the shallow end of the lake parallel to Otley Road on a long timber trestle.

Another locomotive was ordered from Hudswell's, an L.N.E.R. Pacific identical to the Scarborough design, which was given Works No. D582 of 1933 and carried the name **May Thompson** after his wife. A distinctive feature of the extended run was the introduction of a miniature dining car complete with waiters to serve ice-cream to children during the circular tour. For his personal supervision of the line, Thompson ordered an ultra-lightweight four-wheel inspection car which consisted of a pair of bucket seats mounted on a light tubular chassis, the rear axle being driven via a belt drive from a 300 c.c. 'Jap' engine. To complete his train set, a series of scale miniature open wagons were also delivered by Hudswell's.

Stories about Golden Acre during those halcyon days of the early '30s are legion, with its popular attractions including the water chute, boats, cafe and dance floor. One of the best tales must surely be the day a very heavy lady fell in the lake and a gallant male dived in to the rescue, only to find that the water did not come up to his knees! Despite its popularity, the park folded just prior to the 2nd World War, its untimely end putting paid to a new locomotive on order with Hudswell Clarke's that was cancelled in 1938. The locomotive was to have been an oil-fired steam design based on the L.M.S. streamlined 'Coronation' Pacific. It would certainly have been one of the finest miniature locomotives in the country but only got as far as the early stages of construction, never to be completed.

In time, the lines, locomotives and stock were sold to the Blackpool Pleasure Beach Co. who already had a 21 ins gauge system with three Hudswell locomotives. The 'G A P' locomotives were later used on a short line constructed in a small amusement park on the front at Morecambe, opened in 1953, but their condition since then has been far different from the gleaming days in Leeds. The remains of one or two scale open wagons can still be found near the engine shed on the Blackpool line and the re-gauged dining car works in one of the two set trains on the very interesting Pleasure Beach Railway.

Golden Acre retains no visible remains of the line, but has become one of the city's parks with very attractive gardens. The lake is now only a fraction of its original size but is a popular home for water birds.

The Saltburn Miniature Railway

(15 ins gauge)

SALTBURN is now in Cleveland, but when this line was built it was in the North Riding of Yorkshire. Originally owned by the local company, Saltburn Motor Services, this ¾ mile railway was opened in 1948 to connect the seafront at Cat Nab station with the Valley Gardens; apart from a bridge crossing a stream, no major engineering was called for, and sad to relate the line never had any steam locomotion.

It did, however, have one claim to fame with its 4-4-4 tank locomotive **Elizabeth**, a totally freelance steam outline design by Greenly. When completed in 1909 by Bassett-Lowke, it was their sole attempt at internal combustion motive power and was one of the first ever steam outline miniature locomotives built in England. Originally named **Blacolvesley**, it was supplied new to a Mr. Bartholomew, the squire of Blakesley, for service on his estate's private railway in Northamptonshire. As new the power unit was a 12 h.p. N.A.G. motor car engine coupled to a Wicksteed patent gearbox which drove the leading coupled axle via a worm drive up to a maximum speed of 32 m.p.h. The Blakesley Hall railway lasted until 1947, but the tank engine had passed into new hands in 1943, and the new owners re-engined her with an Austin 7 car engine which resulted in a considerable loss of performance. In this revised form it started running on the Saltburn line in 1950, carrying the name **Elizabeth**, but its haulage limitations soon made it stand-by power and for a number of years it languished at the back of the bus garage until finally purchased by Tom Tate of Haswell as a fitting stablemate for his **Little Giant**.

Saltburn's main motive power was a far less attractive but efficient 4-6-2 streamlined Pacific, designed and built by Harry N. Barlow of Southport in 1953. Not the best looking miniature locomotive, it was very loosely based on the famous Gresley A4 profile but without even the luxury of dummy cylinders or any form of valve gear. Despite not conforming to real locomotive practice, it was a solid and reliable machine powered by a Fordson tractor engine coupled to a dynamo, making it a diesel electric, very much in line with modern traction practice. Finished in green livery, it carried the name **Prince Charles**.

Saltburn Motor Services was bought out in 1974 by the Langbaurgh, Middlesbrough & Stockton-on-Tees Joint Transport

Committee which operates under the title 'Cleveland Transit.' The new organisation ran the miniature railway for the remainder of the 1974 season, after which the line and operating rights, together with other associated matters surrounding the boating lake, passed to the Langbaurgh Borough Council. Shortly after the change of ownership, the old footbridge which ran over the valley leading to the 'Italian Gardens' had to be demolished with the result that the track towards the seaward end of the line had to be lifted. At the time of writing, the track is still stacked up by the engine shed but plans are being formulated to re-open the line. The railway never had a fixed timetable, just running to suit requirements from Easter to September each year.

Newby Hall Miniature Railway

(10¼ ins gauge)

SET in the attractive country between Ripon and Boroughbridge on the north-east bank of the River Ure, in over 25 acres of grounds, is Newby Hall, one of the finest and historic of Yorkshire's smaller country houses. Built in the late 1600s to the style of Sir Christopher Wren, the house was later extended by Robert Adam during the 1760s and is now the Yorkshire home of the Compton family. The Hall is renowned for its fine tapestries and superb gardens, and since the house and gardens have been opened to the public they have soon become a popular attraction.

Over the years, the wheel has turned full circle from the days when the large private estates were home to some of the most famous miniature lines, and now it is the stately homes that are re-introducing pleasure lines as an additional attraction and money-making proposition. So it was in 1971 that Mr. Robin Compton created a half mile long, 10¼ ins gauge railway along the secluded bank of the River Ure. The new line was the work of Jonathan Minns of London, an established expert in model engineering matters and a dealer in historic examples of the model engineers' art. The line opened on 4th April 1971, in a blaze of publicity, many of the big 'dailies' covering the event as the opening ceremony was performed by Earl Mountbatten of Burma who, after christening the line's premier locomotive **The Royal Scot,** donned a driver's cap and goggles and at 12 noon prompt drove the inaugural train.

The locomotive, which is still in regular use, is an excellent one-fifth scale model of the London Midland and Scottish Railway 4-6-0 No. 6100 **The Royal Scot**. The prototype had been introduced by the L.M.S. in 1927, the first of 50 built by the North British Locomotive Co. of Glasgow, to work the heaviest and fastest trains, particularly on the 400 miles West Coast main line from Euston to Glasgow, including the long climbs over Shap and Beattock. The Newby 'Scot' was not new to the line but was re-built prior to its journey to Yorkshire. Originally completed in 1950 by the late Stanley Battinson, it was probably the last and certainly the finest of six large scale locomotives built by this competent amateur model engineer, who by profession was manager of Tathams Lace Factory at Ilkeston in Derbyshire. Its early history has been impossible to trace prior to it passing into the hands of Jonathan Minns. At Newby it has not always proved to be the easiest of steamers, but since some boiler work has been carried out by Clarksons of Layerthorpe, York, the locomotive now runs as well as it looks and plays with the six bogie coaches that make up a normal train.

Steam usually works the trains on Sundays and holiday periods. The less hectic weekdays call for the line's more modern motive power which carries the name **Countess de Gray**. In complete contrast to the Royal Scot, this is a Bo-Bo diesel locomotive based on the Western Region of British Railway's main line's diesel hydraulic design, the model being built by Severn-Lamb of Stratford-upon-Avon and powered by a 1600 cc. Ford engine.

One other locomotive has seen some service at Newby but was too small and underpowered for the work, taking the form of a model of a standard gauge 0-6-0 200 h.p. Ruston & Hornsby diesel shunter. Manufactured by Coleby-Simkins Engineering of Stapleford, Leicestershire, its power unit consisted of a single cylinder Triumph two-stroke engine. This machine was later sold to Mr. Terry Stanhope of Leeds, who used parts to produce a narrow gauge diesel design for the Olicana miniature railway at Ilkley, a 12 ins gauge line he subsequently took over.

Newby Hall station is at the foot of the gardens near the river bank and on the river side of the track stands a scale model station building rather similar to one from a pre-war Hornby train set—the nearside platform is a long, wide, flagged surface edged with typical white paled railway fencing. The line follows the river on a private right of way and crosses an old ferryboat slipway by means of a steel bridge. The far end of the line is a balloon loop at the junction of which stands a scale signal box named Bragget Wood, after which the line negotiates the inevitable man-made tunnel. On returning to Newby the locomotive is uncoupled and turned on a turntable, a good time for photography. Well worth a visit particularly on a summer Sunday afternoon, the railway is in continuous use from 2 p.m. and a round trip is 20p per adult passenger.

The Rio Grande Express, Garforth

(10¼ins gauge)

THE latest miniature railway of any size in Yorkshire was opened as recently as 20th May, 1978, by Saville Brothers at their extensive garden centre situated on the Selby Road, six miles from the centre of Leeds.

The very well laid track, with substantial ex-industrial 18 lb. per yard rail on steel sleepers with fine stone ballast, is a credit to the two N.C.B platelayers who carried out the work. The layout is basically two connected balloon loops; the line runs through one of the very large greenhouses, and this forms the main Cactus Junction station, a warm place to catch the train for a 15p ride on a sunny day. The railway, which has an American Western theme, features several level crossings, a girder bridge over an ornamental pool, and of course that essential thrill—a specially created mound to produce a tunnel—all very well executed.

The motive power is one of the now popular petrol hydraulic 2-8-0 steam outline locomotives, based on an American 3 ft gauge Denver & Rio Grande Railroad prototype. Built by Severn-Lamb Ltd., of Stratford-upon-Avon, Warwickshire, it bears the number 278 and a builder's plate with the number 14/5/78, presumably its ex works date of construction, in which case it only just made it in time for the opening of the line. Power is provided by a Ford Cortina engine mounted in the tender, and the livery is black with silver smokebox and polished brass boiler bands. The attractive train has three bogie toastrack coaches, fitted with silver Western style roofs and polished wood slatted seats.

Trains run as and when required and the line is proving to be a popular attraction at what is already a very busy garden centre, especially on spring and summer weekends—a good ride for little boys of all ages!